DISCARD

My Art Class

Nellie Shepherd

DK Publishing, Inc.

LONDON, NEW YORK, TORONTO, MELBOURNE,
MUNICH, AND DELHI

Editor Penny Smith
Designers Melanie Whittington, Jane Horne,
Wendy Bartlet, Lynne Moulding, Victoria Long
Managing Art Editor Diane Thistlethwaite
Production Rochelle Talary
Photography Stephen Hepworth
U.S. Editor Elizabeth Hester

For Jean Gollner (My Wonderful Mom!)

ACKNOWLEDGMENTS
With thanks to: Alfie, Beth, Charlotte, Chelsie, Ciciley, Danny, Edward, Fay, Grace, Heather,
Helena, Holly, Jake, Jessami, Jessica, Kemi, Lucy, Maisie, Mary, Max, Melissa, Mikey, Nicole,
Phoebe, Rebecca, Tessa, and children from Abbeydale School for taking part in the photographs;
Jean Gollner, Anne Lumb, Wendy Morrison, James Pendrich, Melena and Megan Smart
(MMKS Logistics), David Hansel (Memery Crystal), Peggy Atherton, Emma Guest,
Donna Huddleston, Elaine Kowalsky, and Emma Hardy.

First published in the United States in 2003
by DK Publishing, Inc.
375 Hudson Street
New York, New York 10014
03 04 05 06 07 10 9 8 7 6 5 4 3 2 1

Discover more at
www.dk.com

Text and materials copyright © 2003 Nellie Shepherd
"Nellie's" is a trademark of Nellie Shepherd

Illustration and compilation copyright © 2003 Dorling Kindersley Limited

A catalog record for this book is
available from the Library of Congress

ISBN: 0-7894-9579-1

Color reproduction by GRB Editrice, Italy
Printed and bound in Italy by L.E.G.O.

Where to find things

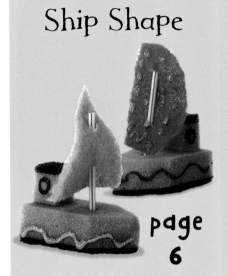

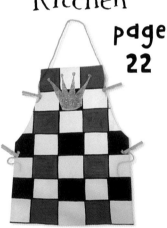

My Art Class

Here is a collection of creative crafts to make with children in your very own art class at home.

It's time to get your friends together and have fun with art! The best thing is that you don't have to spend lots of money to be creative. All the ideas in this book are inspired by materials found in our own kitchens, such as cups, beans, and paper plates. One confession: I did go down to the local store for just a few odds and ends! Have fun and go for it!

Nellie Shepherd

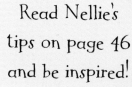

Read Nellie's tips on page 46 and be inspired!

Basic Materials

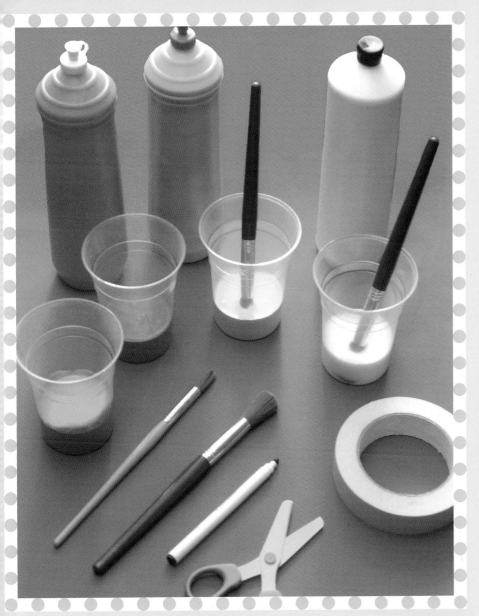

As well as the equipment pictured with each project, you will need the following basic materials:

poster board	cups (for paint and glue)
construction paper	paintbrushes
paint	pipe cleaners
felt-tip pens	play dough
glue	straws
scissors	fabric
stapler	
tape (masking tape is best)	

Keep your art kit in a box so you can find it easily!

Helping hand

All the projects in this book are designed for young children to make, but they should only be attempted under adult supervision. Extra care should be taken when using sharp equipment, such as scissors, staplers, and pipe cleaners, and with small objects that may cause choking. Only use non-toxic, water-soluble glue.

Ship Shape

flat
scourer

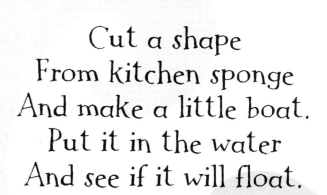

strau

glitter glue

Cut a shape
From kitchen sponge
And make a little boat.
Put it in the water
And see if it will float.

scrubber
sponge

You can use...

scrubber sponges

glitter glue

flat scourers

straws

How to make it!

cut

Cut two corners off a scrubber sponge to make a boat shape. You can glue the cut-off corners onto your boat to make a cabin.

cut again

Cut a flat scourer to make a sail. What shape sail are you choosing? Use glitter glue to decorate—it's so much fun!

thread

Cut two slits—one at the top and one at the bottom of your sail. Thread a straw through the slits to make a mast.

push

Make a slit right in the middle of your boat (but not through the bottom). Push the mast into the hole. Use glitter glue to secure it.

finish

Finish decorating your boat. Then put it on water and have a splash!

Ahoy there!

8

Kid's talk
"I want to make another one for my daddy to play with."
Tom, age 2 ¾

Cool Clips

clothespin

glitter

These sparkly clips
Are the new kind of jewel.
Just wear them anywhere,
And you'll look really cool!

You can use...

glue

glitter

ribbon

clothespins

poster board

Tot Tip! Cool clips make a perfect necklace when you clip them onto a ribbon. Or try clipping them on an ordinary necklace so it looks extra special!

Here we go!

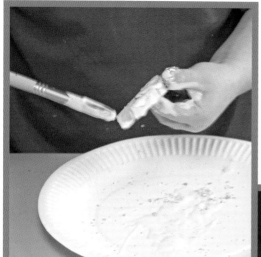

brush

Big party to go to? Forget diamonds! Instead make a set of cool clips! First, brush your clothespins all over with glue.

roll

Roll your sticky clothespins in glitter. Use extra glue and glitter if your clothespins are not completely covered.

clip

Let your clothespins dry, then clip them onto a ribbon. Wear them around your neck, waist, or wrist.

crown

Get really carried away and clip the clothespins onto a strip of card to make a cool-clip crown. It's the tops!

Did you know? The Queen of England's fanciest jewels are called the crown jewels.

Dolly Mixers

Here are two wooden dolls.
Don't they look jolly?
One is named Bill
And the other is Polly.

wooden spoon

I'm Polly!

I'm Bill!

pipe cleaner

pasta

paper napkin

You can use...

cardboard box

yarn

felt-tip pens

glue

pasta

dried beans

napkin

poster board

wooden spoons

pipe cleaners

tissue paper

rice

felt

paint

Tot Tip!

Decorating and dressing your doll is lots of fun— and it's much easier when you lay the spoon flat on the table.

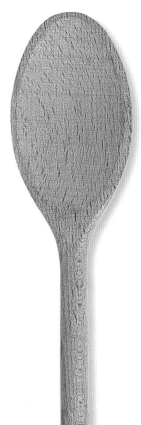

15

How to make it!

paint

Choose a doll to make, or design your own. Now paint the wooden spoon and stick on yarn or rice for hair. Use felt, dried beans, or a felt-tip pen to make a face.

dress

There are lots of ways to dress your doll. You can cut an outfit from poster board and decorate it with felt-tip pens. Or cut out felt clothes and stick them on your doll.

more ways to dress

We dressed Polly in a napkin skirt. Pipe cleaners, tissue paper, and pasta made great belts. We used dried beans for buttons and felt for hands and feet.

make a hat

Our Polly has a little hat made from a cardboard box. You can also make hats from paper cake cases, coffee filters, or whatever else you like!

balloon

yarn

plastic cup

We're going up!

Cup, Cup, and Away!

Take a plastic cup
And tie on a balloon.
Give your little toys a rid
Some sunny afternoon.

18

You can use...

plastic cup

yarn

glue

glittery stars

balloons

tissue paper

Tot Tip! This makes a mega mess! Don't forget to put down lots of newspaper.

You can do it!

blow up

Have fun blowing up your balloon!
Tie on a piece of yarn. Then hang up
the balloon so you can reach all around
it (we hung ours from a clothesline).

stick

Add a little water to your glue.
Tear or cut shapes from tissue paper
and stick them all over your balloon.
Use at least three layers of tissue.
You can add glittery stars (made
from paper and glitter) if you like.

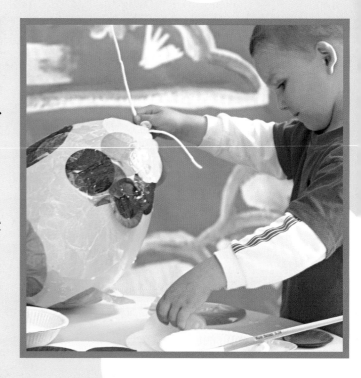

wrap

To make the basket, wrap yarn around
the plastic cup. Attach the basket to your
balloon by taping more yarn under
the basket and to the balloon.
Then find one or two little
passengers to enjoy the ride!

Kid's talk
"I don't want it
to blow away so
I hold it with
my finger."
Ciciley, age 3

King of the Kitchen

You're the king of the kitchen
In your apron and your crown.
You're the best-dressed cook
On this side of town!

glitter crown

clothespin

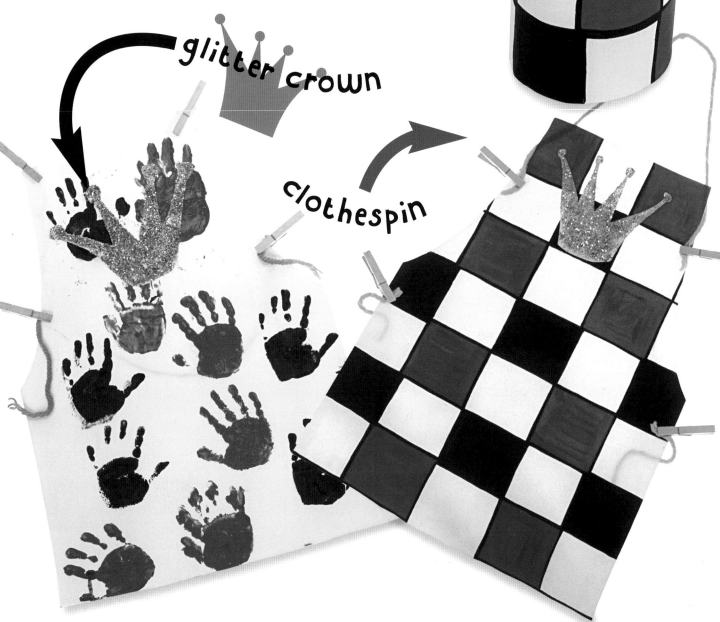

You can use...

glue

yarn

glitter

paint

scrubber
sponger

clothespins

poster
board

kitchen
utensils

Here we go!

cut

Cut an apron shape from poster board. Dip your hands in paint and make handprints, or use a sponge or paintbrush to decorate the apron.

clip

Clip pieces of yarn to the sides of your apron with clothespins so you can tie it at the back. Add a loop at the top for your head. Thread kitchen utensils onto a piece of yarn for decoration— and fun!

cut out a crown

Cut out a crown from poster board and decorate it to match your apron. Use clothespins or tape to hold the crown together. For a finishing touch, make a little glitter crown and stick it on your apron.

ChicKpea ShaKer

tissue
paper

glitter

Shake,
rattle, and
roll!

poster
board

I'm a little chickpea shaker,
And I make a rattling noise.
You can shake me up and down,
And keep me with your toys.

You can use...

plastic cups

poster board

glitter

tissue paper

glue

dried peas or beans

How to make it!

tape

This project is so simple! To make a good musical shaker, half fill a plastic cup with dried peas or beans. Tape it to another plastic cup.

stick

Wrap a half-oval shape of poster board around the plastic cups. Staple the pointed ends in place to make a tail. Stick tissue paper all over.

finish

To finish our chick, we glued on tissue-paper eyes, plus a poster-board beak, wings, and feet. Then we covered her in glitter.

Tot Tip!

Make your chick
and shake along to
Old MacDonald
Had a Farm!

Fantastic Flowers

knives
and
forks

spoons

tissue
paper

This pretty bouquet
Is really fantastic.
You can make your own
With some colorful plasti

paper plate

30

You can use...

paint

plastic utensils

sand

glitter

tissue paper

You can do it!

tape

Tape together the utensils so they look like a bunch of flowers. Stand the flowers in a cup or bowl (you can push them into play dough to keep them from falling over).

paint

Mix paint with a splodge of glue and a little sand. Paint the mixture all over your plastic flowers.

scrunch

Scrunch up little pieces of tissue paper, felt, or whatever else you choose, and stick them onto the painted flowers to look like petals.

roll

Roll a paper plate into a cone to make a vase. Tape it in place and decorate it with paint, glitter, or anything pretty. Fill the vase with your flowers.

Kid's talk
"My flowers
are bright and
they don't need
batteries."
Jessica, age 3

Sweet Belinda

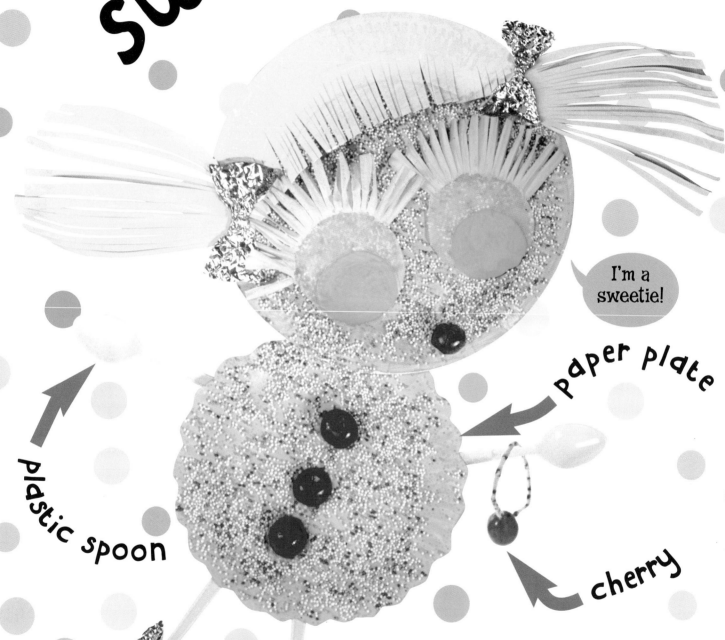

I'm a sweetie!

paper plate

plastic spoon

cherry

aluminum foil

My name is Belinda
And I'm really very sweet.
I'm made from yummy things,
But I'm not for you to eat.

You can use...

food coloring

honey

powdered sugar

plastic spoons

paper plates

wax paper

paper fastener

cherries

Use sprinkles, aluminum foil, or anything you like to make Belinda look lovely. Then let her set in the fridge.

Tot Tip!

How to make it!

mix

Make your own paint by mixing powdered sugar with water and a little food coloring. Make different colors for Belinda's head, body, and hair.

brush

Brush your paint onto Belinda's paper-plate head and body. Scatter sprinkles. Cut out and paint her paper-plate hair and eyebrows.

stick

Using honey as glue, stick on cherries for Belinda's buttons and nose. Stick on and paint her wax-paper eyes. Staple on Belinda's hair and eyebrows.

tape

We used a paper fastener to attach Belinda's head to her body, but you can just as easily use tape. Tape on plastic spoons for arms and legs.

dress up

To dress up Belinda, give her aluminum-foil bows and a cherry handbag made from a whole cherry with a pipe cleaner pushed into either side.

Did you know?
Bees make honey to feed themselves during the winter. As they make more honey than they need, people eat the excess— and artists use it as glue!

Sea-through Sub

straw periscope

whoosh whoosh

yarn

plastic bottle

This little submarine
Likes to hide away.
It dives under the water
And sneaks around all day!

colored tape

cellophane

plastic knives

Yarn

plastic cup

plastic bottle

glitter

gurgle gurgle

Here We go!

soak

First soak the label off an empty plastic bottle. Make sure the bottle is completely dry. Then decorate the outside with colored tape.

stuff

Stuff colored cellophane into the bottle. Then pour in glitter. This is so much fun to do! The glitter sticks to the insides of the bottle with no help at all!

tie

To make the turret, wrap yarn around a plastic cup, then tie the cup to your bottle.

tape

Make a propeller by taping together two plastic knives. Stick them onto the bottle. For a periscope, tape on a straw.

dive!

We poured water into our submarine to help it dive under water.

Did you know?
People work, eat, and sleep in real submarines. They live in them for months at a time!

candy wrapper

Make a wish
at the wishing tree,
And perhaps
it will come true.
Then ask your friends
to come along
And make
their wishes, too.

aluminum foil

twig
sugar

candy

Wishing Tree

You can use...

play dough

plastic cup

Paint

sugar

twigs

paper plate

aluminum foil

candy

candy wrappers

You can do it!

push in

This is such a sweet idea! To make the wishing tree, put a lump of play dough into a plastic cup and push in twigs.

paint

Mix paint with a little glue. Paint the twigs all over, then leave them to dry.

tie

Now make your tree look magical! Tie candy wrappers to the twigs using strips of aluminum foil.

cover

Cover a plate with aluminum foil and put your tree on it. Sprinkle sugar in the cup and all over the plate. Decorate the plate with candy. Now make a wish!

Kid's talk
"This tree grows candy It's not ready yet."
Tom, age 2 ¾

Nellie's Knowledge

I've been teaching my art class to children for over ten years. Along the way, I've discovered a few tips that make the classes lots of fun—and help bring out the creativity in all of us!

Organization
It's good to have all the things you need before you start. But if you don't have something, just improvise and use something else!

Inspiration
Look at all sorts of odds and ends. What can you make them into? Challenge yourself and be inspired!

Fun factor!
Think about inviting friends over to join in. Play music and have a story break. It makes such a difference.

Making a mess

Art is a messy business! Just put down lots of newspaper, relax, and create. It's worth it!

Encouragement

Encouragement is great for building confidence and creativity: one hundred percent encouragement equals one hundred percent creativity!

Positive attitude

We're positive! In my art classes we never say we can't do something, because we simply can!

Making choices

Children's concentration is greatest when they choose the things they want to make. They make their own decisions from the start and they see them through.

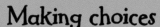

Displaying

Displaying as well as talking about children's art shows it's important. Go on, put it up on the wall!

We've had lots of fun. Good-bye